Information Security for the Business in South Africa

Richard Söderblom

First Publication: April 2015

ISBN: 1508789177
ISBN-13: 978-1508789178

http://www.digitalsecurity.co.za

DEDICATION

This book, "Information Security for the Business in South Africa", is dedicated to my wife, Lucinda Söderblom, who has stood by my side and supported me through all the long hours in assembling this book.

I want to thank my lovely children for simply being the best that they possibly can and making me the proudest father in existence.

THANK YOU

CONTENTS

CYBERATTACKS DEVASTATED MY BUSINESS!

Company: OnlyHonest.com

Michael Hopkins and Cate Costa's startup OnlyHonest.com was just about to hit its one-year anniversary when it became the victim of a nefarious cyberattack.

It was a tremendous setback to the business that was gaining traction with users, social media networks and advertisers, said Hopkins. The website allowed users to debate one another on political topics through video uploads.

In late March, 2013, a group claiming to be affiliated with hacker group Anonymous defaced the website, spreading to every page. When Hopkins tried to get the digital graffiti removed, the attacks escalated. At one point, the hackers were redirecting all of OnlyHonest's traffic to another site.

In May, Hopkins and Costa were forced to take down the website, which already had attracted hundreds of user videos and had 10,000 Twitter followers. The business partners are now struggling to secure funding to make the website secure again before they try to relaunch it.

"We've lost weeks of business and it could cost us thousands of dollars to rebuild the site," said Hopkins. *"We don't have the money but we're not giving up yet."*

"This cyberattack has the potential to completely destroy everything we've been able to build so far," said Costa. *"We hope this isn't the case."*

Company: CreditNerds.com

Eric Counts' customers first alerted him that his website had been attacked in early April, 2013.

"Basically one day I received a huge number of phone calls from people saying that they were getting warning alerts about my site when they were trying to access it," he said.

Malware had infected his website, CreditNerds.com, which helps consumers repair and improve their credit. The malicious code quickly spread to every page.

Although his clients' information, including their dates of birth and Social Security numbers, wasn't compromised, Counts decided to take down the website anyway, opting to change his website hosting provider. He spent R35,000 rebuilding the site.

"My clients were worried about identity theft," he said.

Before the attack, his five-year-old business was getting 10 to 15 new customers a week. That dropped to zero in the 10 days that he was dealing with the attack. He estimates that the cyberattack cost him about R90,000 in lost revenue.

"We're OK," said Counts. *"At most, I've gone a couple of weeks without pay. We're lucky it wasn't worse."*

Company: Mint Green Marketing

When the FBI contacted Alyssa Dver February, 2012, she thought it was a prank.

"They said my website had been compromised and they needed to talk to me about it," said Dver.

Her company, Mint Green Marketing, which she founded 10 years ago, provides marketing expertise to small businesses.

Two FBI agents came to her office to explain that her business website, which primarily provided information about her and her company, had been infiltrated by "really bad people" who were putting malicious codes into her site's file structure. Also unbeknownst to her, security filters had been blocking access to her website.

Dver said the FBI didn't tell her what was in the code or who was involved.

"They wanted access to my site to observe where the traffic was coming from," she said.

The FBI then advised her to rebuild the site, Mintgreenmintmarketing.com, from scratch. The rebuild cost her a few thousand Rand.

"It was very painful," said Dver, who's still feeling the residual effects of the experience: Some internet providers are still blocking the URL for security reasons.

"I could be losing business if potential clients are trying to reach the website but can't," said Dver.

Company: Southwestern Cedar Oil Industries

Eric Erickson's online business selling eco-friendly pest control products was victimized by cyberattacks twice between 2009 and 2013

In 2009, a customer who was trying to buy one of his products informed Erickson that he got a virus alert when he was on his website.

"Back then, we were getting 500 to 700 hits on out site every month," said Erickson. *"I can't imagine how many potential customers saw that alert and turned away."*

Erickson's site was effectively down for four weeks. Then, Google "blacklisted" his site. The search engine began to post a big warning screen when Web users navigated to the site, notifying people that it was infected with malware.

Erickson spent R15,000 to rebuild his site with enhanced security measures. He also spent a considerable amount of time with Google's appeals process to get his site relisted -- a process that took three months.

"The whole experience crushed us," he said *"Our revenue dropped significantly."*

Then, April 2013, it happened again: a virus was detected on the site. The good news was Erickson had purchased technology to contain and get rid of the infection.

"Most small businesses can't afford to spend R15,000 like we had to," said Erickson. *"A single cyberattack can render an online business totally useless, even bankrupt a company."*

Company: CleanItSupply.com

CleanItSupply.com, an online supplier of janitorial and wholesale cleaning products, was scammed out of hundreds of thousands of Rands through a complex scheme involving identity theft and an online scam.

Dan Dillon, founder and president of CleanItSupply.com, said a group of scam artists based in Nigeria used stolen credit card information to order R380,000 worth of supplies from the company's website in March, 2013.

The perpetrators then shipped the supplies to people whom they had recruited to work in a fraudulent work-from-home scheme. The scammers convinced the individuals to ship boxes of the CleanItSupply products to a Texas-based freight-shipping company, which would then send the items to U.S. military personnel based overseas.

Dillon said the freight-shipping company was also a victim of the scam. He first suspected something wasn't right when he spotted a lot of orders coming in for the same products in March, so he decided to call the number on one of the orders.

"I got a funny ring, like the call was going overseas," he said. *"The person who answered didn't speak English well. I asked for copies of the credit card they used and the person hung up."*

It hit Dillon then that his company had been scammed. He quickly contacted the police and was able to trace all of the products before they were shipped overseas.

"It was an overwhelming effort to find the products and then have it shipped back to the vendors," he said. *"That cost us tens of thousands of Rands."*

These five businesses were all victims of recent cybercrime attacks. Not so long ago we thought of cybercrime and hacking attacks only happening to the big players in the world.

In the news we hear of Target being breached and having more than 40 million credit card details stolen along with as much as 110 million bits of customer data stolen. Sony that got hacked and confidential data being stolen that resulted in excess of $100 million.

These are prominently featured but if we look closely we can find thousands of stories that involve small businesses, like the five above. The world is seeing a trend where cyber criminals have identified that small businesses, such as yours, are soft targets.

As small businesses, you don't have the luxury of endless supplies of cash for the latest cyber security wizardry. We need to make the most of limited resources and put in place effective measures that help protect your business, your employees, your clients, and your family.

In this book we will explore the hurdles that small businesses need to overcome in South Africa; both in the form of legislation and the ominous cybercriminal.

In various security reports throughout 2013 and 2014, we can see that South Africa is the 3rd most targeted country for cybercrime, just behind Russia and China.

Most small businesses have little defenses against cyber-attacks and even more are simply not aware of the serious risks imposed by a breach in IT systems and the loss of data.

Let's have a quick look at some statistics from Norton Report for 2013:

➢ 70% of South Africans have fallen victim to cybercrime. This is more than 2 out of every 3 people that use the internet in one form or the other. Globally: 50% of adults fall victim.

➢ About 47% of South African smartphone users had experienced mobile cybercrime in the past 12 months, compared to 38 percent globally.

➢ 49% of consumers use their personal mobile devices for both work and play. This created new security risks for enterprises, as cyber criminals had the potential to access even more valuable information.

➢ 48% of South African social media users have been victims of social cybercrime including:

• 15% of social network users reported someone had hacked into their profile and pretended to be them.

• 25% said they had fallen victim to a scam or fake link on social network platforms.

• While 75 percent believe that cybercriminals are setting their sights on social networks, less than half (44 percent) actually use a security solution which protects them from social network threats and only 49 percent use the privacy settings to control what information they share, and with whom.

- Nearly one-third (31%) of mobile users globally and almost half (47%) in South Africa received a text message from someone they did not know requesting that they click on an embedded link or dial an unknown number to retrieve a "voicemail".

➢ 40% of users globally don't use secure passwords or don't change them often enough.

➢ Every 18 seconds an adult becomes a victim of cybercrime.

In the 2012 edition of the Norton Cybercrime Report calculates the direct costs associated with global consumer cybercrime at US $110 billion over the twelve months of the report.

In South Africa, the costs for the same period amount to R3.7 billion.

This paints a sobering picture of the threat that tech-savvy criminals pose to a small business. In response a number of act's have appeared to help address the problem. Most notably in South Africa are the POPI and PAIA acts that center around safe guarding and use of information.

In the next few chapters we will look briefly at the

POPI Act and what it means for the small business. We will also look at how small businesses are vulnerable and some ways on how we can mitigate the risks.

1: POPI

The Protection of Personal Information Act, No. 4 of 2013 has been made effective on the 11th of April 2014.

This act gives business just one year to become compliant with the deadline currently set for April 2015.

The POPI Act is crafted to help protect personal information and it carries serious penalties for businesses that do not comply. This penalties include either or both of:

1. Up to a R10million fine.

2. Jail time of up to 10 years.

POPI is said to be one of the most comprehensive and well written bits of law in the world that focuses on the protection of information.

POPI is all about regulating the Processing of Personal Information.

Personal Information broadly means any information relating to an identifiable, living natural person or juristic person (companies, CC's etc.) and includes, but is not limited to:

> contact details: email, telephone, address etc.

> demographic information: age, sex, race, birth date, ethnicity etc.

> history: employment, financial, educational, criminal, medical history

> biometric information: blood type etc.

> opinions of and about the person

> private correspondence etc.

Processing means broadly anything done with the Personal Information, including collection, usage, storage, dissemination, modification or destruction (whether such processing is automated or not).

Since this covers the personal information of employees as well, which means that all organisations need to comply with the Act; from government to banks and large corporations through to small home businesses that may only employ one or two staff.

Some of the obligations under POPI are to:

> only collect information that you need for a specific purpose

> apply reasonable security measures to protect it

> ➢ ensure it is relevant and up to date

> ➢ only hold as much as you need, and only for as long as you need it

> ➢ allow the subject of the information to see it upon request

For businesses this means that we need to ensure the safe guarding of all data that is processed throughout the course of business and that contains personal information of clients, users, staff, vendors, contractors, suppliers etc.

This can be a monumental task and with less than a year to comply, this can make you wonder where to start.

2: DANGERS OF CYBERCRIME

Ten, fifteen, years ago cybercrime incidents were not all that common. And these were more directed at large corporations and government agencies. The most we had to worry about were the odd virus or that. A good antivirus software and a basic firewall was all we need for peace of mind in our small businesses.

Today that landscape has changed and a firewall and antivirus program is simply not enough. No longer do we just have to worry about customers, competitors, finances, marketing and all that. We have a new war and a new battlefront and the target is not just you and me but all businesses across the country.

With more and more computers, servers, laptops, smartphones, tablets and other intelligent devices found in businesses so the risks increase. The more data we store, the greater the risk becomes. As our client databases grow so do the personal information we keep on them grow and so do our risks.

If your computer network is compromised, not only will you lose data, personal information, confidential intellectual property which can cost a business thousands if not hundreds of thousands, it can even cause a business to collapse.

Having an infected PC, laptop or tablet on the network cannot just result in data theft, corruption and loss, but it can cause the network itself to be a platform for further attacks against other businesses.

Without the correct tools, training or expertise, you wouldn't even realise that it is happening in your business. The first hint would be the SAPS knocking on the door to confiscate your office computers, servers and other devices. Not to mention that the possibility exists that you, as the business owner, can face criminal charges as well since the attacks have originated from your business network.

This is all above the civil suits and charges you could find yourself in under the POPI Act.

Not to mention identity theft and all the other forms of fraud that could lead to.

Enough doom and gloom, let us take a look at what cybercriminals are after when they target our businesses.

Cybercriminals look for information on your business and your customers. Whether it's kept on servers, is sent through emails or is sitting archived on your employees' desktops, cybercriminals have ways to infiltrate and harvest your valuable data.

Here's a list of what they're looking for:

- Customer records (including contact information, sales history and passwords)

- Contact lists

- Employee Information (including email addresses and passwords)

- Company banking information

- Credit Card numbers

They also want to find a way to:

- Compromise servers

- Infect computers with viruses and malware

- Access your system

- Use your network to attack other computers

So how do they target businesses?

Cybercriminals have developed dozens of ways to exploit the vulnerabilities that may exist in your business. From email scams that target employees to malware that gathers sensitive information, the attacks are complex and effective. Knowing what you're up against will help you protect against it.

Here's a breakdown of the kinds of attacks small businesses can expect to face. This is based on a four-week study of types of attacks participating small businesses experienced:

- Viruses, worms, Trojans: 100%

- Malware: 96%

- Botnets: 82%

- Web-based attacks: 64%

- Stolen devices: 44%

- Malicious code: 42%

- Malicious insiders: 30%

- Phishing & social engineering: 30%

- Denial of service: 4%

This indicates that virtually all small businesses have to deal with viruses, worms, trojans, botnets, and other malware. In fact, this is true for everyone online, from individuals at home to large multinational enterprises.

While less common, web-based attacks, the theft of devices, phishing and social engineering attacks happen often enough to warrant attention. Reducing these threats involves a broader awareness of security beyond just your computer system; it also includes educating employees on cyber security.

Denial of service attacks are rarely reported by small businesses. If you think such an attack is affecting your business, contact your internet service provider for assistance.

3: WHERE ARE YOU NOW?

To know where you are currently with securing your computers, network, data etc. you need to look at:

1. What type of data does my business process?

2. How is that data gathered, used and then destroyed?

3. What are the current implementations to safe guard that data?

Before we can proceed, we must answer the above questions by doing a risk assessment. Once the assessment is done we will know exactly where we are in this point in time and what we need to do to secure the business.

Risk Management is a fundamental approach to the management of a business. While regulations don't stipulate how a business should be secured, it does require that the business be able to prove to an independent auditors that their security and control infrastructure is in place and operating effectively.

In the past IT Security has been seen as the

responsibility of the IT or network staff. Moreover, security risk assessments have typically been performed within the IT department with little or no input from others.

This approach has its limitations. As systems have become more complex, integrated and connected to third parties, the security and controls budget quickly reaches its limitations. Therefore, to ensure best use of the available resources, IT should understand the relative significance of different sets of systems, applications, data, storage and communication mechanisms. To meet such requirements, businesses should perform security risk assessments and include all stakeholders to ensure that all aspects of the IT infrastructure are addressed, including hardware and software, employee awareness training, and business processes.

A comprehensive security risk assessment also helps determine the value of the various types of data generated and stored across the business. Without valuing the various types of data in the business, it is nearly impossible to prioritise and allocate technology resources where they are needed the most. To accurately assess risk, management must identify the data that is most valuable to the business, the storage mechanisms of the data and their associated vulnerabilities.

So how should small to midsize organizations develop their own risk management plan? My recommendation is to follow the steps below to build an understanding of where their IT assets may be exposed and then create a plan to address the gaps.

1. Assess information and infrastructure scope

In this first step, you are identifying the scope of the information systems along with the hardware and software resources and the data that makes up your environment. When looking at the infrastructure, it is important to focus on the critical systems (billing, CRM, HR, legal, knowledge repository, etc). When looking at the data, focus on the "data of concern," including personally identifiable information, HR data, intellectual property, etc.

2. Understand threats and vulnerabilities

Review the threats that face your organization. (These may vary based on your geographical location and your industry.) A threat is the potential for a particular threat-source to successfully exploit a particular vulnerability. List the hardware and software vulnerabilities that exist within your environment. Consider both intentional and unintentional threats. For example, an unintentional threat may be incorrect data entry, while an intentional threat may be a targeted attack via the network or a malicious software upload. The result of this step should be a list of threats with an understanding of their associated vulnerabilities.

3. Estimate the impact

During this step, forecast the adverse impact that could result if each potential threat actually occurred.

The adverse effects of a security event can be described in terms of loss or degradation, or a combination of the following three security goals:

1. Integrity

2. Availability

3. Confidentiality

With these goals in mind, classify the magnitude of the impact. One way to do this is to use a high, medium or low classification, where high has an immediate, critical business impact and low has a relatively limited impact.

4. Determine the risk

Determine the risk for a particular threat/vulnerability in terms of:

a) The likelihood of a threat source successfully exploiting a vulnerability

b) The magnitude of the impact of a threat source successfully exploiting a vulnerability

c) The adequacy of existing security controls for reducing, mitigating or eliminating the risk

During this stage, you should create a risk-level matrix of the risks and the effects (that you classified in step 3.) Again, you can use a high, medium or low classification. A simple starting point is a 3x3 matrix examining threat risks and threat impacts. A sample matrix is shown in the below figure, which includes example threats and possible impact and threat classifications. This matrix will be the foundation of your IT security risk assessment report.

Threat	Impact	Risk
Customer portal behind on system patching by two versions	High	High
Internal billing system has a known software vulnerability	High	Medium
General business admin server needs software version update	Low	Low
Access control on a development server has not be updated in 12 months	High	Medium

While this matrix is hardly comprehensive, I have found few companies that have conducted a security risk assessment process like this to help understand IT risk and vulnerabilities.

5. Plan the controls

During this final step, outline the possible controls that could mitigate or eliminate the identified risks. The goal of the recommended controls is to reduce the level of risk to the IT environment to an acceptable level. These controls can range from people, policy and procedure changes, to new configurations, procurements or the implementation of new technology.

With these five steps, you will have completed a basic IT security risk assessment process. While IT and information security professionals may provide options to mitigate the risks, ultimately it is a business decision and not an information technology / information security decision that is required.

Don't forget to not only look at the cybercrime risk but also physical risks in your assessment. These could include things like:

> **Theft or loss of hardware** - could you cope without key equipment?

> **Fire or excessive heat** - what would happen in the event of a fire? How quickly could you replace damaged equipment, software and data?

> **Water or excessive damp** – it doesn't mix well with IT equipment and if your premises were flooded it is likely that you would have to replace everything.

> **Equipment failure or damage** – like a broken server or dropped laptop.

> **Data theft, loss or disclosure** – perhaps due to poor data security, loss of data-containing equipment or a disgruntled employee – which could result in a significant penalty under the POPI Act.

> **Software failure** – like your business

database or another application.

> **Accidental or deliberate data deletion or corruption** – it's all too easily done if proper security measures are not in place.

4: INFORMATION SECURITY

Information security is the security of data and the systems that collect, store, process, and discard the data.

A business exists solely to fulfill its objectives. Its existence or continued existence is of no use if the business cannot achieve its objectives.

For a business to continue functioning and achieving these objectives, information security has become a non-negotiable necessity.

By keeping a company's business requirements and business objectives in mind while designing the information security strategy will allow it to be appreciated by everybody when it is implemented.

To put it this way; Information technology has to enable information security which, in turn protects the business, its people, infrastructure, applications, customers, and its suppliers.

Essentially information security is the processes and methodologies that protect sensitive information from unauthorised access, use, misuse, disclosure, modification, destruction, or disruption.

The objective of information security is to protect information and its assets such as people, systems, and hardware that use or process, store, or transmit the data. To protect the information and its related systems, business have technology and tools, policies and processes, the needed awareness and training programs, and also rewards for abiding by the security policies and penalties for security breaches Many businesses have disciplinary processes to consider and investigate the security breaches.

Let us have a look at some of the primary aspects that make up information security:

> **Physical Security** plays a big part of any system and cannot be ignored. This is an important line of defense for most businesses.

> **Hardware Security** can form part of physical security even though some of the components can fall under network security.

> **Network Security** is extremely essential in protecting data, especially on the internet.

> **Communications Security** is the securing of communications through the use of various methods. This can be considered broadly as part of network security.

> **Software Security** is another layer that deals with operating system security, application security, and the security of the various software and tools.

> **Personnel Security** is the most important

layer. Keeping staff motivated and aware of the security risks and involving them in the implementation of the security strategy is a very important aspect of information security. Employees, contractors, suppliers and vendors are all important in this regard.

Let us take a look at the primary layers and how they go together in the below diagram.

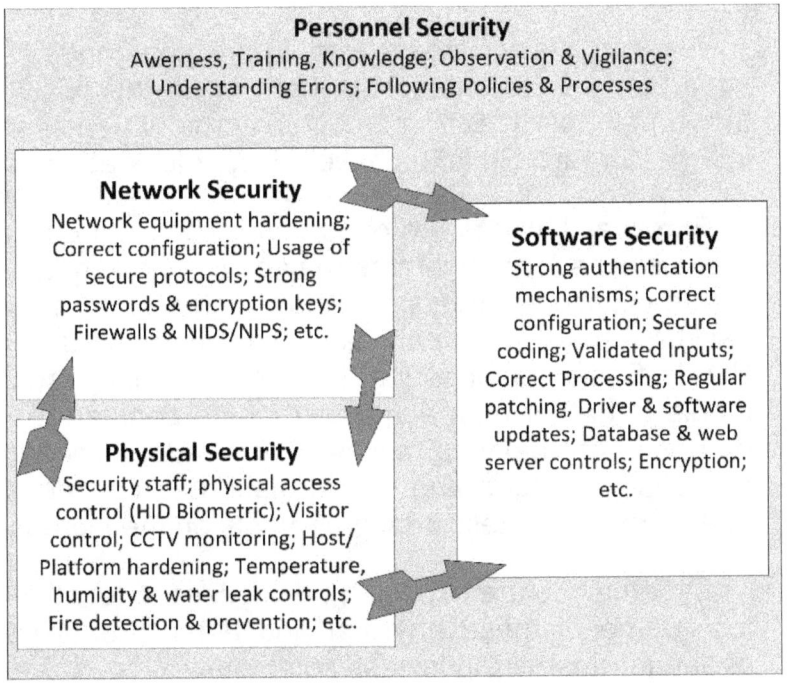

Personnel Security
Awerness, Training, Knowledge; Observation & Vigilance; Understanding Errors; Following Policies & Processes

Network Security
Network equipment hardening; Correct configuration; Usage of secure protocols; Strong passwords & encryption keys; Firewalls & NIDS/NIPS; etc.

Software Security
Strong authentication mechanisms; Correct configuration; Secure coding; Validated Inputs; Correct Processing; Regular patching, Driver & software updates; Database & web server controls; Encryption; etc.

Physical Security
Security staff; physical access control (HID Biometric); Visitor control; CCTV monitoring; Host/ Platform hardening; Temperature, humidity & water leak controls; Fire detection & prevention; etc.

An effective information security strategy should consider all the layers without omitting any of them.

Security Threats

In information security 'threat' means anyone or anything that poses a danger to our businesses data and information, the computing resources, or users. The threat can come from outside or inside the business. Studies show though that around 80% of breaches come from insiders.

We can class threats into many categories. An important way to categorise them is on the basis of the "origin of threat", namely external threats and internal threats. So let us have a closer look at these.

External Threats are ones that come from outside the business. These threats may be physical, network communication threats, human threats such as hackers, software threats, and legal threats such as POPI. Social engineering threats like using social media to gather data and impersonate people for the purpose of gaining access or fraud. Theft of personally identifying information, confidential strategies, and intellectual property is on the increase.

Cybercrimes are exposing businesses to legal risks too. Some of these physical and legal threats may endanger an entire business completely.

Below we can see some of the important external threats.

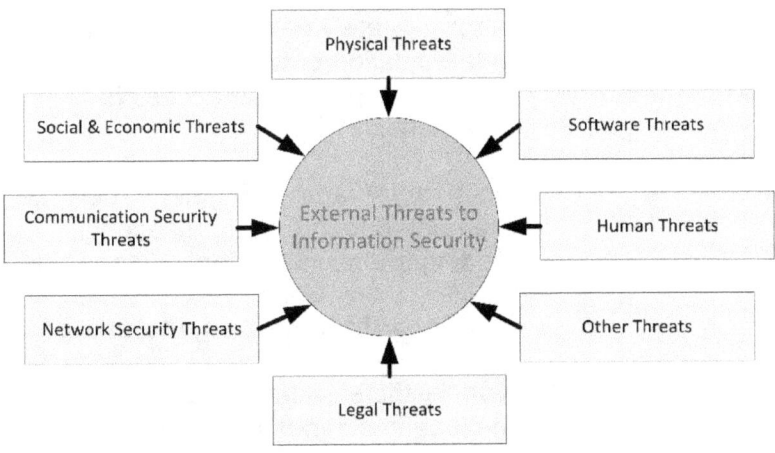

Internal Threats are threats that come from inside the business.

Primary contributors are suppliers, contractors, and employees. The major threats are misuse of information, the destruction of information, and of cause fraud. When we look at the reasons why people commit cybercrimes inside of companies that they work we find that the reasons are:

> **Weak or no security policies, including:**

  ❖ improperly classified information or unclassified information that leads to the intended or unintended sharing of confidential information with others.

  ❖ Undefined or inappropriate access to customer resources or contractors / suppliers that lead to fraud and theft.

  ❖ Inadequate separation of duties leading to fraud and misuse.

❖ Inappropriately defined or implemented authentication or authorisation which leads to inappropriate access to information.

❖ No clear hierarchy of "gatekeepers" who are related to information security, leading to assumed identities and roles.

➤ **Weak security administration, including:**

❖ Non-restricted administrative access on the local machines and/or network that leads to misuse and infection of the systems.

❖ Weak user passwords allowed in the system and applications, leading to unauthorised access and information misuse.

❖ Weak administrative passwords being used leading to compromised systems and stolen data.

❖ Non-restricted access to external media such as USB or personal devices, which leads to theft of data and infection of systems.

❖ Non-restricted access to employees through personal devices or from unauthenticated networks, leading to data theft.

❖ Unrestricted access to contractors and suppliers leading to theft or misuse of information including through dumpster diving or shoulder surfing.

- ❖ Unrestricted website surfing, leading to infections of viruses, phishing, or other malware.

- ❖ Unrestricted remote access leading to unauthorised access or information theft.

- ❖ Accidentally deleting data permanently.

➢ **Lack of user security awareness, including:**

- ❖ Identity theft and unauthorised access due to weak passwords.

- ❖ Not following company policies, such as appropriate use of assets, clean desk policy, or clear screen policy, leading to virus attacks or confidential information leakage.

- ❖ Divulging user IDs and/or passwords to others, leading to confidential information leakage.

- ❖ Falling prey to social engineering attacks.

- ❖ Falling prey to phishing and similar attacks.

- ❖ Downloading unwanted software, applications, or images or utilities/tools leading to malware, viruses, worms, or Trojan attacks.

- ❖ Improper email handling/forwarding leading to the loss of reputation or legal violations.

- ❖ Improper use of utilities like messengers

or Skype and unauthorised divulgence of information to others.

❖ Inappropriate configuration or relaxation of security configurations, leading to exploitation of the systems.

❖ Entering incorrect information by oversight and not checking it again or processing the wrong information.

❖ Ignoring security errors and still continuing with transactions, leading to the business being defrauded.

As we can see from the above, there is greater risk of damage to the information, data, and systems in our businesses from internal threats than there are from external threats.

The list above is far from complete!

With this in mind we will be looking at some of control methods that we can deploy to help mitigate some of the risk.

5: CONTROL TYPES

We employ different control to reduce RISK.

Remember that:

*"**Risk** is the **Possibility** of a **Threat** exploiting a **Vulnerability** in turn causing **Loss**"*

In the context of information security we are concerned about our information system. This includes:

➤ The servers

➤ The networks

➤ The clients

➤ The applications

➤ And everything that runs in that space

To help us reduce risk to our business and the information that our business collects and processes, we use three different types of controls:

1. Technical

2. Management

3. Operational

When looking at the control types, we want to implement them to best preserve the CIA of the assets of our information systems.

CIA is the **Confidentiality**, **Integrity**, and **Availability**.

A threat is something that would compromise either the confidentiality, integrity or availability of our business assets.

A vulnerability is a weak point, which could be something like a wireless access point that doesn't have any authentication or encryption. A threat takes advantage of the vulnerabilities in the business network and could cause theft of information (the loss of Confidentiality) or if the business data could be manipulated somehow (the loss of Integrity).

If an attacker used a threat to compromise a point of weakness and then launched a denial of services attack (DOS attack), that would lead to a loss of Availability of the network and or information in the business.

We make use of the three different types of controls to mitigate risk (think of a countermeasure to the CIA threat).

Keeping with the above example, if on the WiFi access point, we secured that with 802.11i and enterprise authentication, then we have mitigated that risk with the open access point that anybody could log onto and threaten our CIA.

The threat is still there (somebody that wants to log onto our access point) but since we improved the security on it the risk is now less. In other words the potential of someone getting on that access point has been reduced.

The reasons we use controls is to reduce risk and primarily that will involve implementing counter-measures and removing vulnerabilities in our network systems so that the potential threats have a reduced opportunity to be affective against our systems.

Technical controls would include things like:

> Implementing an access control list (ACL) on our firewall to limit access in and out of our network.

> Using 802.11i encryption, also known as WPA2, on our WiFi access points.

> Special systems such as intrusion prevention systems (IPS), malware scanners, anti-virus, application aware firewalls.

Management type of controls are also sometimes also referred to as administrative controls and this normally includes such as:

> Getting someone in to assess the risks in the information systems.

> A written security policy is also a management control.

> Planning and reviewing different controls is

in itself a management control.

Operational controls deal with the day to day procedures and policies that people should follow to maintain the overall CIA of the organisation. For example, a change management or procedure to prevent changes on the network, servers, or systems from impacting the business.

We will find that in any company that is doing security correctly there are a number of policies. These include:

Acceptable Use Policy – gives the guidelines as to what is and is not allowed on the networks and systems. This is also known as the AUP.

Privacy Policy – is concerned with the collection and release of information in the business and also usually documents the types of information collected and used.

Security Policy - states in writing how a company plans to protect the company's physical and information technology (IT) assets. A security policy is often considered to be a "living document", meaning that the document is never finished, but is continuously updated as technology and employee requirements change.

Mandatory Vacation Policy – by forcing an employee to take a two or three week holiday at least once per year reduces collusion and fraud. The idea is that the employee has no contact at all with anyone in the business (no phone or email communication at all). This makes it easier to identify if an employee is involved in activities that could jeopardise the business such as embezzlement or neglect of duties or security procedures.

Job Rotation Policy – ties up with the mandatory vacation policy in that it assists in picking up on anomalies that may be happening. It also allows multiple people to develop a similar skillset, which aids in reducing risk should an employee leave the company or be involved in an accident or such.

Separation of Duties Policy – is a must to reduce the risk of fraud. An example would be that the business has a requirement to pay vendors and so forth. We would then have the following groups of employees that have the ability to:

1. Requisition a payment

2. Load the payment onto the banking system

3. Approving the payment

No single person should have the ability to do all of the above.

The AUP and Privacy Policy are very important and should be given to each employee at least once per year to ensure that they know about and understand how to maintain the CIA of the business systems. A good idea would be to incorporate this into the employees and reviews and have them sign it saying that they are aware of the policies and understand them and will abide by them.

6: SECURITY AWARENESS

Let us look at some ideas that need to be trained and communicated to everyone from the lowest employee through to senior management.

When looking at companies that do security awareness training, there are really only two types.

1. One is the company that is just interested in ticking the box that says done and getting it out of the way. The problem is that these trainings are not that affective and rarely stick.

2. The other type of company cares and understands why it is important that the staff get security awareness training. These companies follow up and gather training metrics to validate the staff actually understand the training and can implement the techniques that are presented to them.

Having formal training is very important and not just to the staff but to the middle and senior management and even the executive management. Everyone in the business needs to participate in security awareness training.

Security awareness training is a major contributor to reducing risk.

It allows employees to know and understand the various security policies and procedures in the company.

An example would be having a staff member, Jack, that is aware of things such as **Personally Identifiable Information** (PII) and he is aware of how sensitive that information is and how important it is that that data not be leaked out or disclosed in unauthorised ways. If Jack sees something that might compromise the confidentiality of that information, the security awareness training can help the Jack to respond and help reduce a data leak of that sensitive information.

A good way of doing training is doing **role based training**. This allows employees to get a better understanding of the security associated with different roles. It also role cross training or role reversal training, which in itself helps prevent any person from having a role so critical that the business ceases to function should anything happen to that person.

Information Classification or Label is really important in certain businesses and it is important that employees understand this.

Examples of classification are:

> High

> Medium

> Low

Or:

> ➢ Confidential

> ➢ Private

> ➢ Public

Mandatory Access Control (MAC) essentially permits specific employees to have specific clearance to access specific data.

For instance, Jane has a clearance of medium. This allows her to have access, or be able to read or write, information that has a classification of medium or low.

The only way that staff will know about the classification of the data and the proper use of that information would be through security awareness training.

Another important aspect of security awareness is the use of social networking and peer-to-peer (P2P) and how it can compromise security.

There are also things like learning about new threats and new security trends and alerts.

Employees don't just learn this by default but become aware of it and learn how to implement policies and procedures through a comprehensive and effective security awareness training program.

Proper security awareness training should also encompass the correct use or handling of the information or data in the business. This will also include the proper disposal of information that is no longer required. This is especially important for media devices. Employees should know that they cannot just through a hard drive, CD or DVD or USB memory drive in the trash as this can have a serious breach of the CIA and cause large amounts of data to be leaked.

Just as paper documents are shredded or burnt, so should devices that store data be physically destroyed.

Another aspect of security awareness training should be compliance with various laws. Best practices in the industry and standards within the industry of the business.

One of the most importance focuses of training should be on user habits. This will include:

> **Passwords** – Have complex passwords that are changed regularly and never allow anyone else access to your password.

> **Data handling** – How do you handle the data in your day to day activities?

> **Clean desk policies** – Don't leave paper documents with sensitive data lying around on your desk.

> **Workstations** – Make sure that your computer is always locked when leaving your desk.

> **Prevent tailgating** – When going through security doors, don't allow other employees

to slip through with you without providing the proper authentication.

> **Personally owned devices** – Have company email on your phone or tablet? Be careful. It will be considered a severe breach of CIA if the device should get lost or stolen and it is not encrypted with a strong password or able to be wiped remotely.

As we can see, security training should not be a matter of simply getting it done but should be designed so that it suits the particular business and the information that is collected and used in the business. Above all it should ensure that all employees understand what is at RISK.

7: EVOLUTION

It is a constant fight when it comes to securing your business's data and information.

Cybercrime is finding new ways to attack networks and steal information or disrupt services on a daily basis. It is up to us to continually innovate and implement new methods to stay ahead of the game.

It is a game that we cannot afford to lose. If we fall behind and our business systems are comprised, we stand a very real chance of a major setback as a best case and worse case our business will be shut down. Permanently.

Is not staying abreast of the game worth the risk for your business? Is it worth the gamble that your business won't be maliciously attacked? This choice is up to you.

This book is meant as a short overview from a business owner's perspective into information security. It is far from comprehensive as that would take many more pages and chapters which will lead to you having to spend much more time reading, which could be used by starting to secure your information.

If you would like to find out more about how to secure your business's data and what options or training programs are available for you, please contact me through the website dedicated to this book:

http://www.digitalsecurity.co.za

In the meantime I have included two bonus chapters that will be very helpful when planning the security policy for your business.

Thank you for reading this book.

Richard Söderblom

BONUS CHAPTER: SOCIAL ENGINEERING

The weakest link in any security system is always the human factor, therefore I think it is imperative that I include a chapter on social engineering.

Social engineering refers to a non-technical type of attack that relies solely on human interaction and mostly involves tricking other people to give up sensitive information. Think of a con-man as an old school type of social engineer.

Let's look at an example:

Jane works at a company, ACME. Kate is a new employee that just started at ACME.

Kate's sole purpose is for social engineering to gain company secrets and information. Maybe for future attacks or to sell to a competitor.

Let us look at some techniques that Kate might use.

Shoulder Surfing. Evolves looking over the shoulder of someone while they are working. Maybe Jane is busy entering some user information. It could be her username and password to log onto the company domain or her email. Maybe Kate walks past Jane as she puts in a pin code that unlocks a door.

See where security awareness training can fit in here?

Dumpster Diving. Jane printed out an email to refer to during a meeting. Afterwards she throws the paper into her trash. Later Kate walks past and picks up that paper.

What was on that email printout? Was it PII (personally identifiable information)? Was it sensitive financial information? Possible new client information? Could even be last year's company directory.

That information that is thrown away could be on an optical disc such as a CD or DVD. It may contain irrelevant information or it might be very relevant for a competitor.

Tailgating. Kate has been watching a building for a few days and recognises that a number of employees take regular smoke breaks.

She then prints out an ID badge for her similar to the others and goes over to smoke and mingle with the other employees. Kate then follows them in to the building and doesn't have to swipe her access card because someone else already has.

Now that Kate has access to the building she can plant things like flash drives with malware on it and so forth.

Impersonation. John is busy at his computer and Kate walks over and says:

"Hi. We have just finished the upgrades of XYC for our computer systems and we need access to your computer for about 30 minutes to finish it and test."

If John says that is ok, then we have a problem.

It might also be that Kate disrupts service to John's computer. She then hangs back and waits for John to call the helpdesk and when he hangs up, goes over and says, "Hey I was just in the area and they asked me to come over and see what your problem might be."

Kate has now impersonated a support staff member and will probably have full access to the computer that John is logged on to.

Whaling. Whaling is very similar to phishing over email with the difference being that they are going after bigger targets.

Here Kate is sending an email to the company execs in an attempt to have the execs click on links and so forth that could compromise those individual user accounts or information.

Hoaxes. On the internet there are thousands of hoaxes. For example you can be looking at a website and get a popup message saying that your computer is full of viruses or that it is running slow and you can speed it up by clicking here.

A hoaxe could also be an email about some serious virus or something bad that could happen. It almost always has a link to a website that says they can protect you or fix the problem for you.

In this case Kate contacts Paul, Jane's manager, and convinces him that there is a serious issue on the system and that she urgently needs further access into the system to fix it. If successful, Kate could end up with Paul's credentials with which she could get further into the network.

Since we are human is what makes social engineering so affective in compromising businesses.

There is a psychology of persuasion that can be used against us and that is why social engineering works so often. Here are some reasons:

> **Concept of Authority**. People generally do what they are told if they think a person of authority has told them to do it.

> **Consensus**. Also known as social proof. As a general rule, we want to do what other people are doing. As humans we highly value social proof.

> **Urgency or Scarcity**. This is a very powerful way of getting people to provide information that they would not normally provide.

> **Familiarity or Trust or Liking**. We want to do things for people that we like. If someone

befriends us for malicious purposes and gains our trust or we start liking them then they will most likely be able to get information from us that we would not otherwise give out. An example would be reciprocity, we want to give back.

One common problem that I see is that if a person that has malicious intent somehow gains login credentials, either through social engineering or other methods such as weak passwords, that person can gain a lot of information simply by logging into the company's web base email system such as Outlook Web Access (OWA). OWA is normally accessible from anywhere in the world through any standard web browser and just requires a user's Window's or domain username and password.

BONUS CHAPTER: INFORMATION SECURITY RISK ASSESSMENT CHECKLIST

Since a big part of implementing an information security policy or plan is knowing the risks that are in your business, I have included this basic high-level risk assessment which you can tailor to fit your particular business's operations.

	Yes/No
A. Organizational and Management Practices	
1. **Security Program Governance** – Executive Management has assigned roles and responsibilities for information security across its organization. This includes, but is not limited to, the following: documenting, disseminating, and periodically updating a formal information security program that addresses purpose, scope, roles, responsibilities, applicable laws and regulations, and the implementation of policies, standards, and procedures.	
2. **Confidentiality Agreements** – Implement confidentiality or non-disclosure agreements with contractors and external entities to ensure the agency's needs for protection of classified information is met.	

3. **Risk Assessments** – A review process at planned intervals is implemented to ensure the continuing suitability and effectiveness of the agency's approach to managing information security.	
4. **System Security** – A formal document that provides an overview of the security requirements for agency information systems and describes the security controls in place (or planned) for meeting those requirements is maintained.	
5. **System Certification** – An assessment of the security controls in place for existing systems and those planned for new systems is conducted at least once each year. Assessment tools are readily available through security organizations, like National Institute of Standards and Technology (NIST), SysAdmin, Audit, Network, Security (SANS) Institute, and other reputable sources. The agency's ISO reviews and approves actions taken to correct any deficiencies identified. Responsible technical or operational management are included in the review process.	
6. **Configuration Change Control** – Changes made to information systems are controlled and documented. The changes are reviewed and approved in accordance with written policy and procedures, including a process for emergency changes.	
7. Security Categorization – Procedures to classify systems and information that is stored, processed, shared, or transmitted with respect to the type of data (e.g., confidential or sensitive) and its value to critical business functions are in place.	
8. Vulnerability Scanning – A regular occurring (e.g., bi-annual, quarterly, monthly) process using	

specialized scanning tools and techniques that evaluates the configuration, patches, and services for known vulnerabilities is employed.	
B. Personnel Practices	
1. **Security Awareness** – Training is provided to all employees and contractors on an annual basis that addresses acceptable use and good computing practices for systems they are authorized to access. Content of training is based on the agency's policies addressing issues, such as, privacy requirements, virus protection, incident reporting, Internet use, notification to staff about monitoring activities, password requirements, and consequences of legal and policy violations.	
2. **Human Resources Security** – Policies and procedures that address purpose, scope, roles, responsibilities, and compliance to support personnel security requirements, such as access rights, disciplinary process, etc. are in place.	
3. **Position Categorisation** – Procedures for identifying system access needs by job function and screening criteria for individuals performing those functions are in place.	
4. **Personnel Separation** – A process to terminate information system and physical access and ensure the return of all agency-related property (keys, id badges, etc.) when an individual changes assignments or separates from the agency is developed and implemented.	
5. **Third Party or Contractor Security** – Personnel security requirements for third-party providers and procedures to monitor compliance are in place. Requirements are included in acquisition-related documents, such as service-level	

	agreements, contracts, and memorandums of understanding.	
6.	**Personnel Screening** – Employee history and/or a background check is performed on employees who work with or have access to confidential or sensitive information or critical systems.	
C. Physical Security Practices		
1.	**Physical and Environmental Program** – Policy and procedures that address the purpose, scope, roles, responsibilities, and compliance for physical and environmental security, such as security perimeter and entry controls, working in secure areas, equipment security, cabling security, fire detection and suppression, room temperature controls, etc. are in place.	
2.	**Physical Access Monitoring** – The need for monitored access to business areas is evaluated. In monitored areas, records for approved personnel access and sign-in sheets for visitors are maintained. Logs are periodically reviewed, violations or suspicious activities are investigated, and action is taken to address issues.	
3.	**Physical Access Control** – Physical access to facilities containing information systems is controlled and individual's authorization is verified before granting access.	
4.	**Environmental Controls** – The necessary environmental controls, based on a requirements assessment, which includes but is not limited to backup power to facilitate an orderly shutdown process, fire detection and suppression, temperature and humidity controls, water damage detection and mitigation are provisioned	

and properly maintained.	
5. **Secure Disposal of Equipment** – Processes are in place to permanently remove any sensitive data and licensed software prior to disposal.	
D. Data Security Practices	
1. **Disaster Recovery Planning** – A Disaster Recovery Plan (DRP) is in place that supports the current business continuity needs of the agency. The DRP plans for the recovery of technology and communications following any major event that disrupts the normal business environment, provides for periodic updating and testing of the plan, and its documentation includes, but is not limited to:	
• Recovery based on critical and sensitive business needs.	
• Location of regular backups of systems and data, with documentation.	
• Regularly updated information about where copies of the plan reside, including appropriate off-site locations.	
• Training for appropriate personnel.	
2. **Information Back-up** – Backup copies of information and software are completed on a routine schedule, tested regularly, and stored off-site.	
3. **Monitoring** – System logging, and routine procedures to audit logs, security events, system use, systems alerts or failures, etc. are implemented and log information is in placed where it cannot be manipulated or altered.	

4. **Data Classification** – Policies and processes to classify information in terms of its value, legal requirements, sensitivity, and criticality to the organization are in place.	
5. **Access Controls** – Policies and procedures are in place for appropriate levels of access to computer assets. Access controls include, but are not limited to:	
• Password management, including the use of strong passwords, periodic password change, and restriction of sharing access and/or passwords. System access is authorized according to business need and password files are not stored in clear text or are otherwise adequately protected.	
• Wireless access restrictions are in place, with organizational control over access points, prohibition and monitoring against rogue access points, appropriate configuration of wireless routers and user devices, and policy, procedure, and training for technical staff and users are in place.	
• Secure remote access procedures and policies are in place, and are known and followed by users.	
• Mobile and portable systems and their data are protected through adequate security measures, such as encryption and secure passwords, and physical security, such as storing devices in a secure location and using cable locking devices.	

• The tracking of access and authorities, including periodic audits of controls and privileges is in place.	
• Networks challenge access requests (both user and system levels) and authenticate the requester prior to granting access.	
6. **Least Privilege** – Configuration to the lowest privilege level necessary to execute legitimate and authorized business applications is implemented.	
7. **Data Storage and Portable Media Protection** – Policies and procedures to protect data on electronic storage media, including CDs, USB drives, and tapes are in place. Procedures include labels on media to show sensitivity levels and handling requirements, rotation, retention and archival schedules, and appropriate destruction/disposal of media and data.	
E. Information Integrity Practices	
1. **Identification and Authentication** – Policies and procedures for identification and authentication to address roles and responsibilities, and compliance standards are in place.	
2. **User Identification and Authentication (typically userid and password)** – Information systems/applications uniquely identify and authenticate users when it is appropriate to do so.	
3. **Device Identification and Authentication** – Information systems/applications identify and authenticate specific devices before establishing a connection with them.	
4. **System and Information Integrity** – Policies and procedures for system and information integrity to address roles, responsibilities, and compliance	

standards are in place.	
5. **Malicious Code Protection** – A regular patching process has been implemented to protect against malicious code. The process is automated when possible.	
6. **Intrusion Detection** – Tools and techniques are utilized to monitor intrusion events, detect attacks, and provide identification of unauthorized system use.	
7. **Security Alerts and Advisories** – The appropriate internal staff members receive security alerts/advisories on a regular basis and take appropriate actions in response to them.	
8. **Secure System Configuration** – The security settings on systems are configured to be appropriately restrictive while still supporting operational requirements. Non-essential services are disabled or removed when their use is not necessary as to eliminate unnecessary risk.	
9. **Software and Information Integrity** – Information systems/applications detect and protect against unauthorized changes to software and information.	
10. **Information Input Accuracy, Completeness, and Validity** – Information systems/applications check data inputs for accuracy, completeness, and validity.	
11. **Flaw Remediation** – Information system/application flaws are identified, reported, and corrected.	
F. Software Integrity Practices	
1. **System and Services Acquisition** – Policies and	

procedures for system and services acquisition are in place to address roles and responsibilities, and processes for compliance checking.	
2. **Software Integrity Practices** – Policies and procedures associated with system and services acquisition and product acceptance are in place.	
• Acquisitions – Security requirements and/or security specifications, either explicitly or by reference, are included in all information system acquisition contracts based on an assessment of risk.	
• Software Usage Restrictions – Controls or validation measures to comply with software usage restrictions in accordance with contract agreements and copyright laws are in place.	
• User Installed Software – An explicit policy governing the downloading and installation of software by users is in place.	
• Outsourced Information System Services – Controls or validation measures to ensure that third-party providers of information system services employ adequate security controls in accordance with applicable laws, policies and established service level agreements are in place.	
• Developer Security Testing – A security test and evaluation plan is in place, implemented, and documents the results. Security test results may be used in support of the security certification process for the delivered information	

system.	
G. Personal Computer Security Practices – Personal computing devices include desktops, laptops, notebooks, tablets, Personal Device Assistants (PDA), and other mobile devices.	
1. **Device Hardening** – Operating system and application level updates, patches, and hot fixes are applied as soon as they become available and are fully tested. Services on the computing devices are only enabled where there is a demonstrated business need and only after a risk assessment.	
2. **Lock-Out for Inactive Computing Devices** – The automatic locking of the computing device after a period of inactivity is enforced.	
3. **Data Storage** – Data that needs additional protection is stored on pre-defined servers, rather than on computing devices, for both data protection and backup/recovery reasons. Confidential, sensitive, and/or personal (notice-triggering) information is not stored on computing devices without a careful risk assessment and adequate security measures.	
H. Network Protection Practices	
1. **Network Protection** – Network and communication protection policies and procedures are in place. These documents outline the procedures to authorize all connections to network services. Authorization is based on an evaluation of sensitive or critical business applications, classification of data stored on the system, and physical location of the system (e.g., public area, private access, secure access, etc.).	

2. **Boundary Protection** – Equipment designed for public access (i.e. Web servers dispensing public information) is protected. These are segregated from the internal networks that control them. Access into internal networks by authorized staff is controlled to prevent unauthorized entry.	
3. **Protect and Secure Network Infrastructure** – Policies and procedures for technology upgrades, network equipment (e.g., servers, routers, firewalls, switches), patches and upgrades, firewall and server configurations, and server hardening, etc are in place.	
4. **Transmission Integrity and Confidentiality** – Data is protected from unauthorized disclosure during transmission. Data classification is used to determine what security measures to employ, including encryption or physical measures.	
I. Incident Response Practices	
1. **Incident Response** – Incident response policies and procedures consistent with applicable laws and state policies are in place. These include but are not limited to identification of roles and responsibilities, investigation, containment and escalation procedures, documentation and preservation of evidence, communication protocols, and lessons learned.	
2. **Incident Reporting** – Proper incident reporting policies and procedures are in place. These include training employees and contractors to identify and report incidents, the reporting of incidents immediately upon discovery, and preparation and submission of follow-up written reports.